YANTRAS
OF
WOMANLOVE

YANTRAS OF WOMANLOVE

images by **TEE CORINNE**

text by **JACQUELINE LAPIDUS**

introduction by **MARGARET SLOAN-HUNTER**

THE NAIAD PRESS, INC.
1982

Printed in the United States of America
First Edition

Cover design and title page by Tee A. Corinne

Typeset by C & H Publishing Services
        Shelburne Falls, Massachusetts

ISBN: 0-930044-30-4

For Caroline

foreword

Four springs ago, when a woman I was deeply and irrationally in love with moved out, I began to have waking dreams about this book. It became like a lover for me through one of the most difficult winters I have known as an adult—sustaining me and giving me a reason to go on.

In November of that year, while visiting Jacqueline Lapidus in Paris, I read a poem she had written called "Design for the City of Woman." The structure and sequence of the poem offered a way to order and bind the separate pictures together and has been a constant source of inspiration.

Some of the individual images date from as early as 1975 when Victoria Hammond asked me to make photographs for her to work from in illustrating *Loving Women*. This was the first time I had ever photographed lovemaking and the energy and excitement I drew from the experience would inform my work for years. Additionally the tremendous positive response to the *Sinister Wisdom* cover and poster (Issue 3, 1977) convinced me that sexual imagery is important and needed within our lesbian communities.

A large part of the story of *Yantras* involves other people. Once upon a time (1972, age twenty-eight) I was getting ready to kill myself. Like many suicidal people I was also looking for a way to affirm life and continue living. Bob and Mary Goulding (teachers, therapists and generally wise people) understood my dilemma and helped. Some time later I was wondering if my time might be better spent as a therapist than as an artist. Mary Goulding's comment that there are lots of good therapists and not very many good artists was the decisive factor in my choice of how to use my skills.

Yantras took much longer to complete than I had expected, of course. It did not grow in an orderly way. There were periods of passionate involvement and others when I could not imagine that it would ever become a reality. Some women have been especially helpful to me in clarifying my vision: JEB (Joan E. Biren), Jane Rule and Corbett O'Toole. Ollie's support and Margaret Sloan-Hunter's encouragement have repeatedly moved me through stuck and scared places and helped me see my work as important and healing to others. The word *yantras*, which means diagrammatic representations of fields of energy, was located by Frances Doughty in a tantric yoga book after I told her I needed a word like mantra but for images instead of sound. Finally, more than sixty women volunteered to be photographed. Without their participation this book would not exist.

I have questioned often whether I wanted to thank or even mention my mother whose death gave me enough money to free some of my time from teaching and other income-producing activities. My relations with her ended in six years of struggle and a final four of silence yet *Yantras* is a book which, had she lived, I believe she would have been proud of.

• • •

Yantras is about the spirituality of sexuality, the transcendence that can take place when making love to ourselves and others, the repetition of action through which pleasure is sustained and release is possible. The patterns that grew like snowflakes, like the sound of rain, still surprise me. The organizing principle within the book is Baroque* like the South I grew up in: full of details, running on and on, overflowing. I share her with you with love.

Tee A. Corinne, 1982

---

*For a discussion of Southern Baroque see Mab Segrest's "My Mama's Dead Squirrel, and Southern Humor" in *Feminary* XI:3, pp. 8-25.

introduction by
MARGARET SLOAN-HUNTER

introduction

My first lovemaking experience with a woman was in August 1970, in West Des Moines, Iowa. I had spent the entire month before that in Cuernavaca, Mexico, with twenty-nine other women and children living in an intentional feminist community. All of us—except "The Lesbian Couple"— were actively heterosexual, but because of our experience in this second wave of the feminist movement, we had already begun to feel a new love and appreciation for ourselves and other women. For some of us, those feelings were intensified by the day-to-day experience of living, sharing, confronting, studying and growing together.

The days were spent educating ourselves and being exposed to our surrounding culture, meeting with local feminists and sharing communal meals. In the hot evenings, which usually followed a daily afternoon rain that made the nights more fresh and tolerable, we had study groups whose topics ranged from women in China to racism. Each of us shared her particular expertise. One of us had gone to Cuba with the Venceremos Brigade. Some women had participated at the first Women's Liberation Conference held near Chicago in the late '60s. There was a Karate expert from Tennessee who held daily sessions.

Attendance at the study sessions varied, but on the night "The Lesbian Couple" talked about lesbian lifestyles, all of us heterosexual "liberals" were present. An important, and for some of us, first discussion on our own sexuality took place. Our spirits were high and our defenses surprisingly low, and it was on that evening that I consciously felt and knew that I was attracted to Pat, who sat across from me in our circle of sisterhood. I felt her respond to me also, and on the rooftop of the old monastery where we all boarded she acknowledged that she was indeed turned on to me. We decided, however, not to "do it" there. There was no privacy; we all slept in bunks. So we would "do it" when we returned to the States—although we were not quite sure what "doing it" with another woman even meant.

It is important to understand that we were not sexual novices, especially me. I had been heterosexually active since the age of eight, and even at that moment was a wife and the mother of a three-year-old child. Pat also could boast of an active sexual history. But we still didn't know what to do with each other.

The most vivid memory that I have of the evening in West Des Moines is not of our actual lovemaking attempt but of our conversation before it. We both expressed honest ignorance. As a sexually active girl and later as a wife I had found sex good—but predictable. There had been variations of the theme, but the theme itself remained basically the same. Now Pat and I were facing each other on a bed. There was no penis, no male aggressor to initiate and show the way. She agreed with my assumption that our sexual fulfillment with each other, and with other women in the future, would never be as good as it had been with men, but that we would get a lot of *emotional* sustenance!

The irony of this impresses me to this day. Who should know better than two women what to do with each other to arouse, stimulate and excite to orgasm? A large part of the problem was our basic ignorance of our sexual selves—commonplace among women of our generation, whose lives were filled with sexual experience coupled with sexual ignorance. But an even larger part was having no images in our own minds of what we could possibly do with each other in bed. Even the staid medical journals presented pictures—but not of lesbians. All of the "How To . . ." manuals and books were heterosexual. Women-loving-women imagery was nowhere to be found.

The closest I had come to fantasizing woman-to-woman intimacy was while still in Mexico, lying on my bunk one afternoon. I created a hazy (naturally) scene of two women lying naked in the sand (at night, of course), with a gentle ocean breeze flowing smoothly over their bodies. In the background was the soft strum of a Spanish guitar! This was all right for characters from Central Casting or some kind of artistic portrayal, but it lacked what was necessary to connect my mind with what my body was feeling. I never even imagined that women could engage in oral sex or vaginal penetration. I had no image of women lying bare, fondling each other, French kissing, being sensual and passionate. Neither did Pat.

So we left the experience somewhat frustrated sexually, but definitely more curious and convinced that lesbianism had promise and possibility. A year later, we arranged for our paths to cross, and this time we were able to give each other the benefit of what we had learned from more experienced sexual partners.

Today, after a decade of active lesbian sexuality, I still feel a certain sadness and anger about our first "coming out" experience. It would have been decidedly better had we not been so ignorant of our sexual selves and each other. There we were—both having breasts and vaginas, both having clitorises—and not knowing what we could do! The problem was not just Pat's or mine. Many other women like ourselves had no guidelines, no references and no visual images. Unless you were lucky enough to come out with an experienced lesbian you were left on your own.

All women, heterosexual and lesbian, have suffered from the lack of accurate information—indeed, negative information—about our sexual selves. If masturbation was "dirty" and surely not something to talk about, how much more "dirty" it must be to touch another woman "down there" in a "nasty" way! How equally "bad" to even write about lesbianism, conceptualize it in a poem or song, or portray it in an artistic, sensitive way.

Heterosexist society has defined the lesbian by her sexuality rather than dealing with the woman as a whole. When not identifying lesbians as "man-haters," and daughters of cruel fathers who beat them, or women who couldn't get a man, our socie-ty has chosen to define lesbians only in terms of sex. Lesbians are supposed to be consumed by sex, performing lewd acts and engaging in licentious conduct, insatiable nymphomaniacs. One wonders how daily tasks like cooking, cleaning the house, shopping, raising children and holding a job could be squeezed into such a consuming sexual schedule. Lesbians are supposed to know all about sex, and this might be true of some lesbians. For many of us, however, sexual awareness, like consciousness, keeps growing all the time.

The assumption that lesbians know it all leaves little room for growth. Many oppressed people have fallen victim to the stereotypes that surround their group. As a black man, my father has suffered all of his life for not having natural rhythm, just like a lesbian who has been highly active sexually but is embarrassed to admit that she has never had an orgasm.

For the first issue of *Ms.* magazine in July 1972, the editors decided to excerpt a chapter of the book *Lesbian/Woman* by Del Martin and Phyllis Lyon. The chapter chosen was "What Do Lesbians Do?" That, then radical, decision resulted in the loss of much needed advertising dollars and cancellations by some charter subscribers. But as the editor who had "come out" publicly as a lesbian, I received many letters from lesbians across the land; some who had been lesbians for years and others who had not yet slept with a woman, but knew they would. For some that chapter was a starting point, for others an opportunity for comparison. The response confirmed my suspicions that I had not been alone in my initial ignorance and hunger for information about and confirmation of lesbian sexuality.

This experience made me quick to accept an invitation to be one of the speakers at a sexuality conference sponsored by the New York City chapter of N.O.W. in the early 1970s. I decided to expose myself, to talk about how experienced and yet how ignorant I had been about my own sexuality, and how I was still learning. I had always talked freely and candidly about sex and sexuality, so many of the participants were surprised to hear the "liberated" lesbian reveal that she had not masturbated until 1972, two years after I first made love with a woman, five years after the birth of my child, and seventeen years after my first sexual intercourse. The women were surprised but relieved. I didn't mind exposing myself to that large audience, mostly strangers, because I knew I was not alone. Lesbians discussed problems, some that had weighed on them for years, interfering with potentially good sex lives. Many revelations and discoveries were made that day, but the overwhelming desire expressed was for lesbian erotica—posters, pictures and films to educate, stimulate and validate.

●

Lesbian erotica is new. In 1971, the film *Holding* by Constance Beeson exposed many women to female lovemaking on film, even though the film was done by a heterosexual woman. Laird Sutton, a heterosexual man, made the fifteen-minute film *In Winter Light* in 1974. Both of these films provided visual erotic stimulation, but not until Barbara Hammer's film *Dyketactics,* also in 1974, did lesbians see explicit lesbian erotica made from a lesbian perspective. In 1975 the book *Loving Women* by the Nomadic Sisters made its important debut. The book was filled with "how to's" and drawings. It could be called the first lesbian sex manual. Women all around the country began to swap notes, see images and get ideas for improving techniques. Even the lesbian who "knew it all" could have a point of comparison for all she knew. The fact that this book was so necessary and so well received is a statement in itself. Lesbians—the salacious, sex-crazed nymphomaniac know-it-alls—were devouring a "how to" manual.

The book coincided with the rising affirmation of lesbian sexuality. Later in 1975, the book *What Lesbians Do* by Godiva showcased lesbian erotic art and poetry. That same year the *Cunt Coloring Book* by Tee Corinne called on women to reclaim images of our genitals, and encouraged us to pick up crayons and color our self-defined erogenous zones.

Ann Hershey's 1976 movie *We Are Ourselves* was done as educational media for National Sex Forum, San Francisco. This color film shares with us, in voice overs, two lovers' awareness of their lesbian sexuality. It stimulates and arouses as well as educates and can be viewed as an artistic portrayal of lesbian erotica by lesbians.

The frustrating thing for many lesbians is that most of these erotic images have been of the young, white, able-bodied and thin. While we continue to expand our sexual consciousness, it is important that our images reflect who we really are. It is easy to fall into the traps of a sexist world, limiting our portrayals to a very small group.

The scene of lovemaking between older women in the book *Sister Gin* gave many of us a first-time sensual, tasteful and stimulating counter to the assumption that women are dried up after fifty. This myth must be exploded because our own reality tells us it is not true. The fat woman has been somewhat better represented, but images of flat, tight stomachs, narrow hips and small breasts still predominate. The disabled lesbian has had virtually no reflection in erotic images. Like the larger society, the lesbian community has assumed that disabled women are nonsexual beings. But there are many disabled lesbians and their erotic images must be included not only for self-validation and stimulation, but for raising the consciousness of able-bodied women. Lesbians of color have been confined to the monotonous images of either gun-bearer or baby-bearer. There still exists, in the world and in the lesbian movement, a myth surrounding the sexuality of all these women, resulting in a hands-off policy when it comes to erotic representation. But lesbians are of every color, size, age and physical description and our erotica must reflect that range.

Women's sexual oppression is political. It is no accident that, as we embark on the decade of the 1980s, our reproductive rights still cannot be taken for granted and freedom of sexual expression is outlawed in most states. It was design rather than mishap that women were told (and believed) that the female orgasm was vaginal—that we needed a penis inside us to be orgasmic. This gave credibility to the myth that lesbians, who do not have sex with men, are unfulfilled, sexually frustrated spinsters—which is far from the truth.

●

Lesbians in the feminist movement, whether in the closet or out, have been the pioneers and liberating factor in much of what goes on with women today, and sexuality is no exception. It has been lesbians, who most times found the heterosexual guidelines unworkable and unacceptable, who paved the way for all women to explore, question, discover and share, thereby expanding female sexual awareness.

Lesbian erotica is important, if for no other reason, because it portrays women-loving-women from the lens, pen or brush of the woman who knows what that experience is and feels like. The lesbian erotic artist must not be viewed as a pornographer, because her culture, perspective and consciousness are completely different. She portrays images that are sexual, sensitive, stimulating, erotic and passionate. She has the right and privilege of reflecting back to lesbians sexuality as she knows, sees and lives it.

Tee Corinne, lesbian, feminist sex counselor, researcher, artist and photographer, is one of the pioneers of the New Lesbian Erotica. For the better part of a decade she has researched and created images of lesbians in lovemaking and intimate portraits. Her positive attempt to be inclusive in her subjects is reflected in her pictures. I have long admired her courage as well as her art. She has the ability to relax her participants—all raised in a society that makes women feel ashamed of their bodies—in order to capture the naturalness and the sensuous beauty of a moment that might never be expressed again. She does not just point the camera and shoot; she directs the camera, captures and gives back, reflects what is real. As a result there is trust and no feeling of exploitation.

I speak for the fat, black lesbian who at thirty-two was still ashamed of her body, but who reluctantly agreed to be photographed for this book. She saw her image, and smiled as she looked at the proofs. She no longer feels uncomfortable with the light on when she is making love.

Margaret Edmondson Sloan-Hunter
August 1979

YANTRAS
OF
WOMANLOVE

images by **TEE CORINNE**
text by **JACQUELINE LAPIDUS**

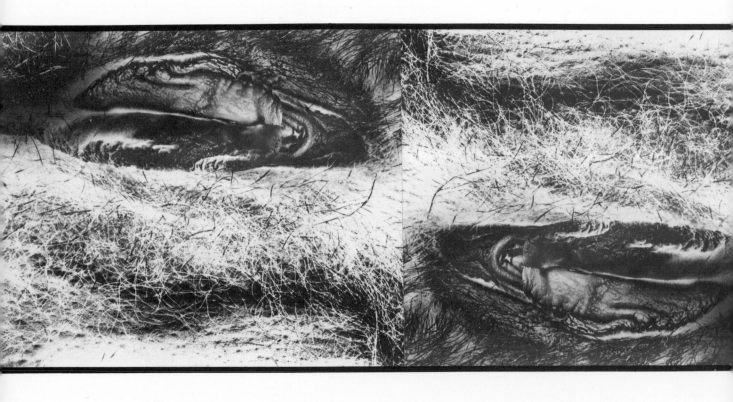

I

a newborn conch
sparkles on wet sand
no bigger than a grain of rice
already
she knows how to secrete
her own house

II

Walking along the shore at low tide, I came to a place where the cliffs were white with salt, as if the tears of an entire continent had dried in an instant on the rock's flushed face. Above the high-water mark was a row of irregularly shaped holes in which birds nested; above these, the earth was brick-red, and at the summit tufts of wild rosemary, thyme and fern thrust their heads into a hazy sky. As I stood admiring the wheeling flight of the gulls, I heard music coming from the next beach. I climbed over a shelf of mossy rocks, following the sound, and stumbled into the entrance to a grotto worn away in the cliff. The sun had not yet set. Late afternoon light slipped violet into the grotto and fell upon a circle of women sitting around a slab of rock that jutted out from the cavern wall.

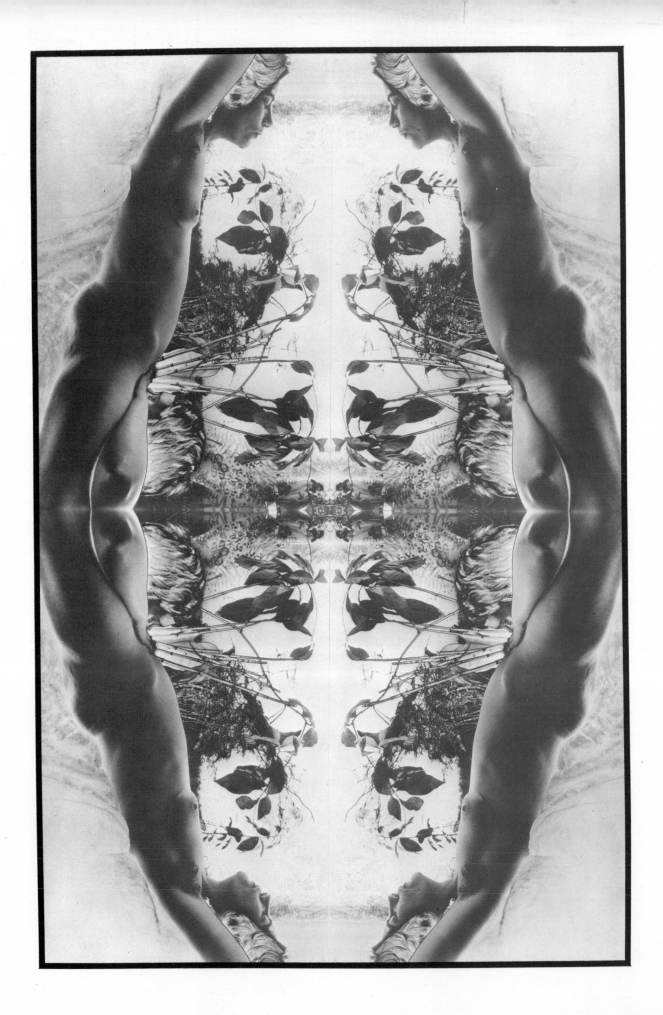

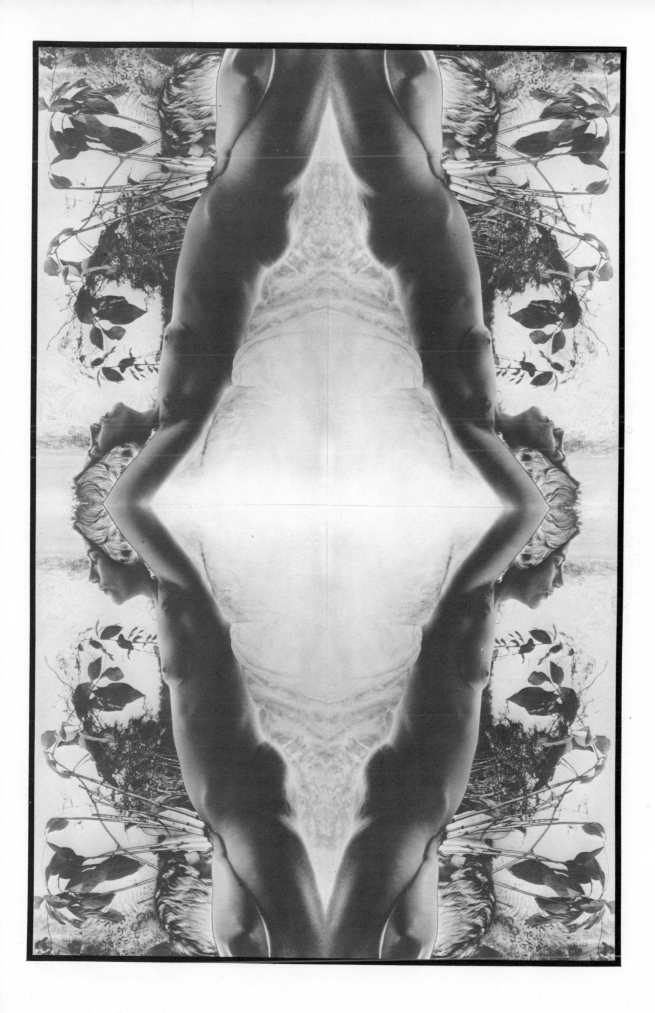

The women were not surprised to see me. They moved over to make room for me at the table. In the center of the table was a tide-pool filled with mussels and clams. One of the women dipped her hand into the pool and scooped up several fresh clams with fluted shells which she offered to me. I pulled one from its shell with my teeth and swallowed it live; it slipped easily down my gullet, and in a few seconds I felt a warm, insistent throbbing between my legs as my clitoris emerged from its bed of wet moss. The women smiled at me and began to sing, in a language strangely familiar. I lay down naked on the rock ledge with my buttocks in the tide-pool, my arms and legs outstretched. The women leaned over me. Their cool fingers stroked my hands and feet, then my nipples and my clitoris. One woman slid her tongue slowly into my cunt, and I felt a great wave surge through my entire body.

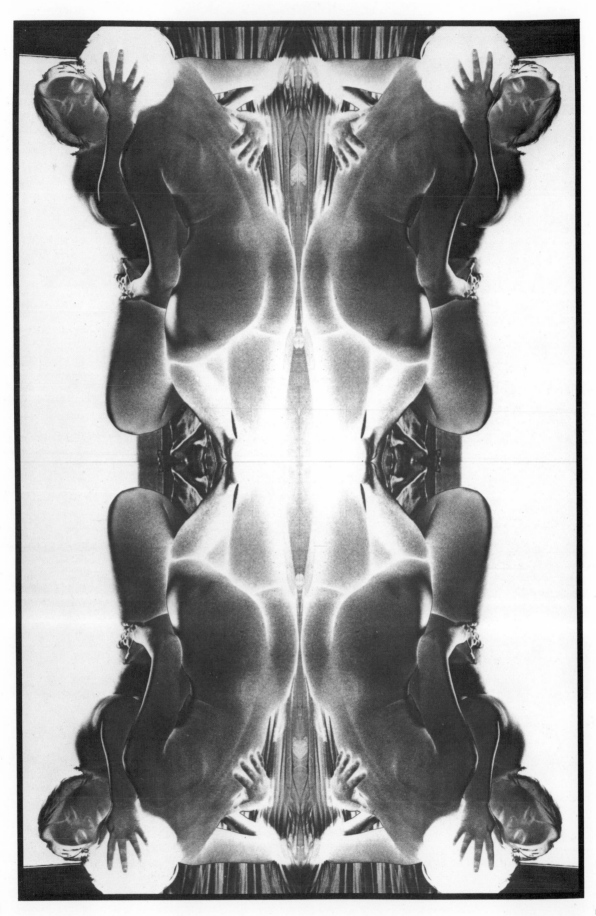

III

concerned   we are concerned
we have always been alone together
we have always confided in one another
we have always found time to whisper
amongst ourselves concerning our concerns
long ago we learned to speak to each other
with borrowed cups of sugar
singing as we washed our blood
from endless sheets and towels
nourishing each other with perpetual
soup   concerned   we have
always been concerned
for centuries our cheeks have brushed
each other's cheeks   at weddings
funerals   fairs and church bazaars
we have tasted each other's tears
laying out corpses
we have stroked our sisters' bellies
and held our daughters' hands
and sung to their screams, and drawn
babies gasping from their wombs
concerned   we are always concerned
oh yes   we are used to one another
bearing our burden together, struggling
for a common cause: our own survival
and now we are doing it
openly   for ourselves

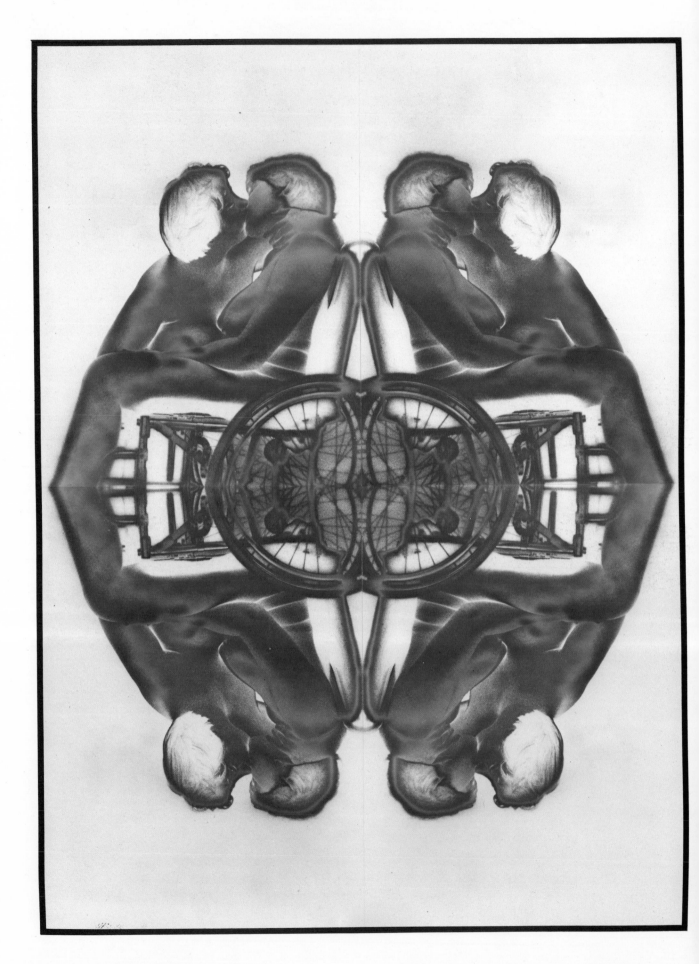

IV

I can only say things in the ways I know, but I am open,
and see farther every day. I am exploring the shadows of
myself, and my fingers reach out to touch you and learn
the pattern of your web.

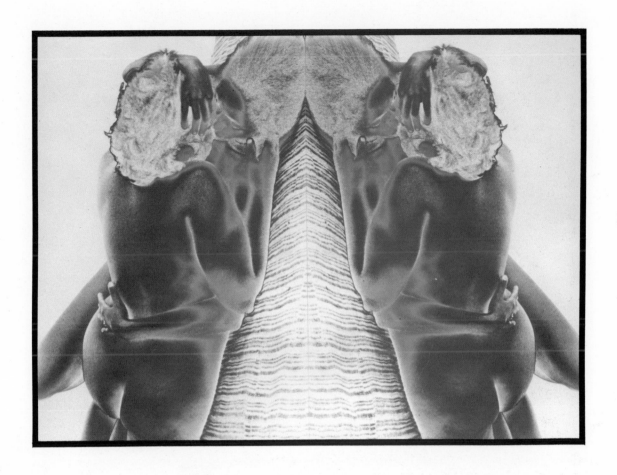

I want to become like you, strong, lithe, healthy. I long to conceive as you do, concentrating womanenergy upon the womb, stimulating the ovule to duplicate then multiply, cells proliferating like laughter made flesh. I dream of being pregnant among women, caressing each other's bellies to prepare the child for community. I imagine giving birth close to the earth, squatting, my friends holding me as I breathe, blow, grunt in rhythm with you, while you sing to encourage me, stroking my body to ease the child's passage. I feel my baby lying on my belly, bathed in sun-warmed sea water, your fingers gently massaging her until she begins to smile. I contemplate our nursing, each woman offering her breast to the others' babies. I delight with you in the taste of our nipples, in the pleasure that flows like milk from your bodies into mine.

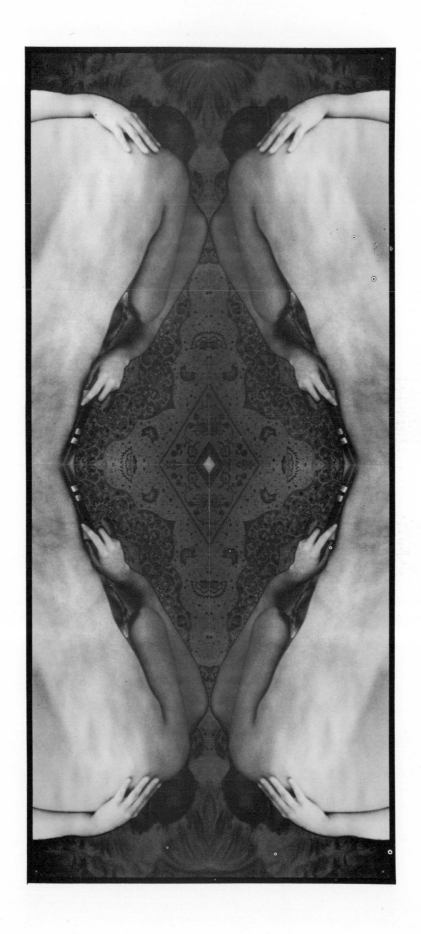

38

One of the women links arms with me and we stroll along the beach, watching the little girls build labyrinths in wet sand.

"We have lived together for so long," she tells me, "that nearly all of us menstruate at the same time. During the menstrual period we feel particularly strong and exuberant. The power of our blood surges through us. We squat on the beach and study the patterns made by our blood on the sand, for these reveal secrets of the inner self and help us to intimate knowledge. At night, we celebrate our sisterhood in ritual. We draw the blood from one another's cunts with our fingers, then paint our bodies with it. Images of pleasure flow from each woman onto her partners' face, breasts, belly and buttocks. Then we dance in spirals, singing, linked to one another in the vortex, symbol of perpetual motion. Older women who no longer menstruate, excited by caresses, secrete enough cyprine to paint their bodies. Although the designs are colorless on their wrinkled skin, everyone can see them clearly."

40

V

Dear Catherine, the message
you could not then transmit to us
has nonetheless arrived
as surely as if etched with acid
on the moon's dark side
   spreading like bacteria
     nourishing as bread
       decoded in our guts
absorbed into the very tissues of our being
and suddenly appearing
as sweat, saliva, blood, cyprine:
women's language of love

> *"the words of the poems dance across the page,*
> *the birds in the air dance above the clouds,*
> *the fish in the water dance among the waves"* °

Let us leave the drones to build cities
Let us play with each other like ribbons of light

° Emmett Jarrett, *Design for the City of Man*

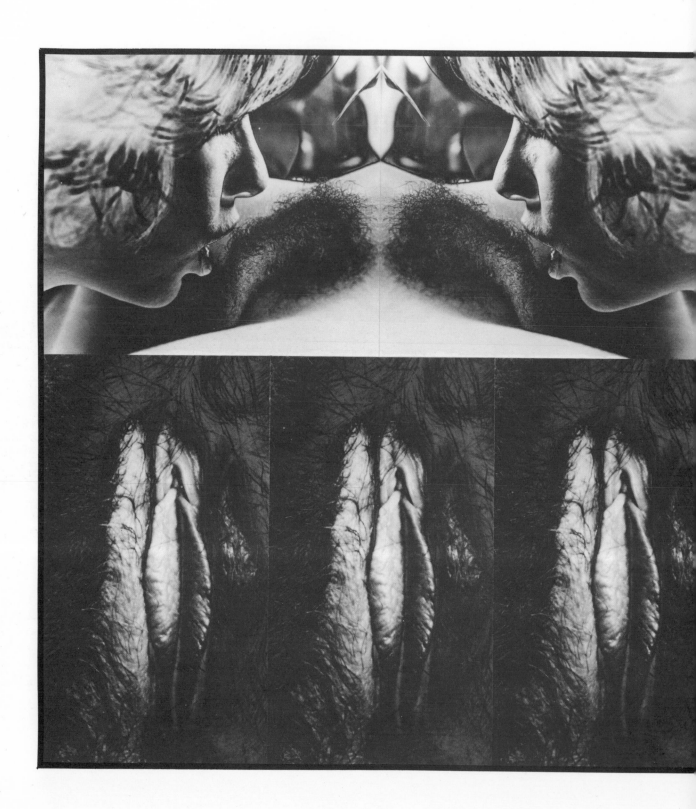

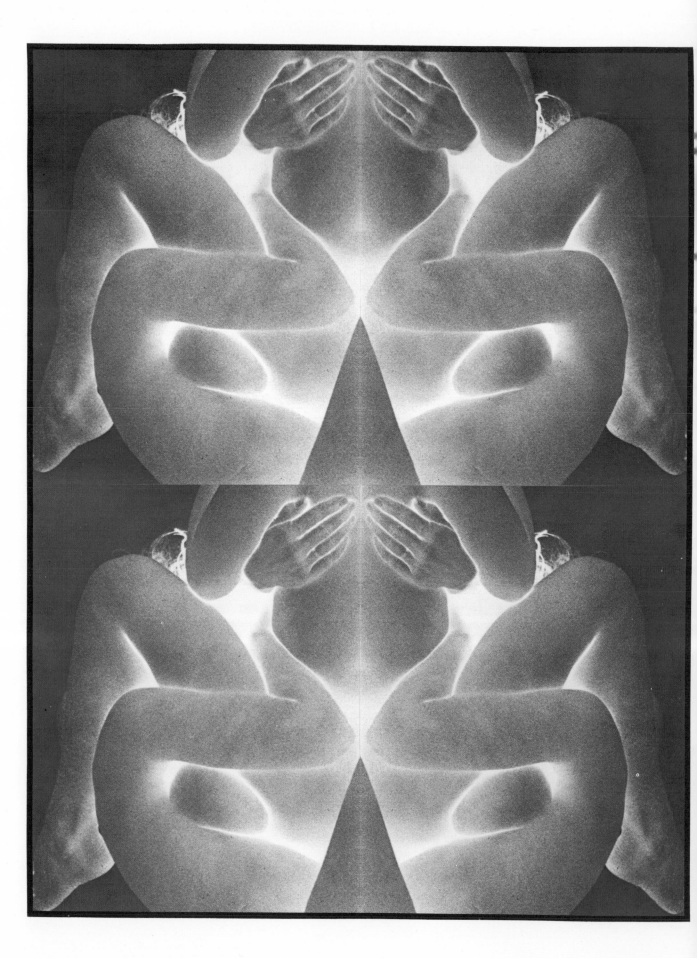

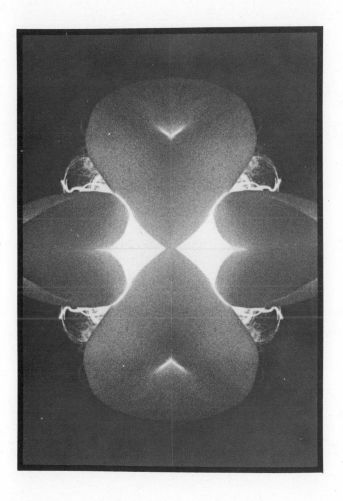

VI

I have become friendly with Catherine Blake, the mystic engraver whose visions were stolen from her and distorted for publication. Her images remain in my mind even when she is elsewhere. Sometimes she speaks in a wordwind of sounds. The women here are developing a new language, for although we have become a people capable of reproducing ourselves, we cannot consider ourselves a nation until we share a mother tongue. We expect this to take several centuries.

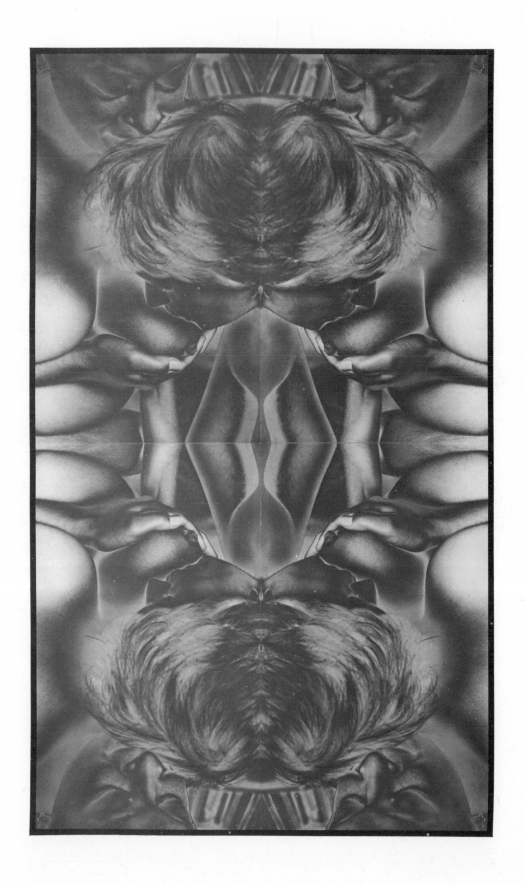

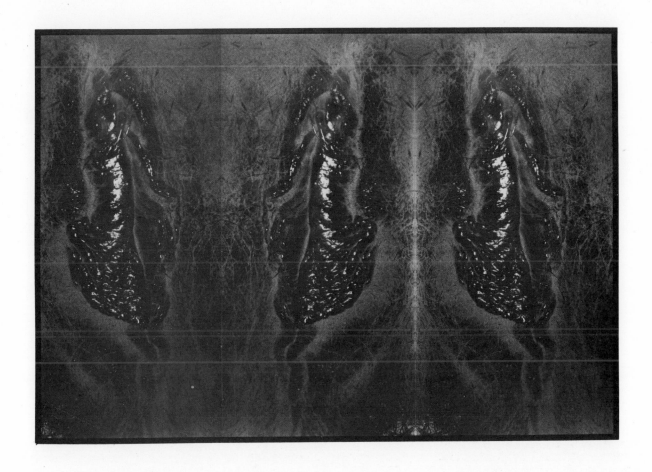

"We live," says Catherine, "in the crevices, the hollows, the spaces, the secret places, we live on the edge of the wave. The tide never goes out exactly as she came in—she always leaves us something we can use."

Another day she observes, "The little mermaid's error was not that she longed for feet, but that she paid for them with her voice. Also remember Philomena, whose tongue was torn out so that she could not testify she had been raped. We too must transform ourselves into nightingales and soar."

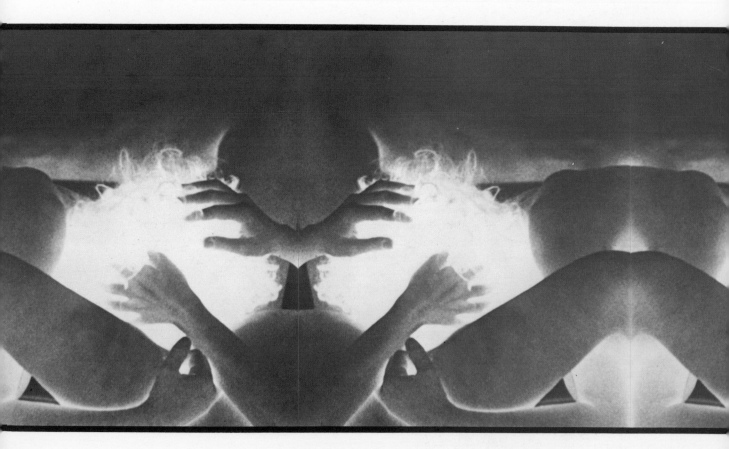

We are lying on the sand where the sea curls onto the shore. The water is green and so clear that every pebble on the bottom is visible. Catherine and I are lying together in the warm ripples watching tiny shells wash over our feet, idly playing with each other's hair as it floats between our legs. Transparent fish dart up to our bare thighs and nibble at us. Suddenly the sun turns into a flaming circle and sinks behind the cliff, leaving a trail of fire behind her in the sky.

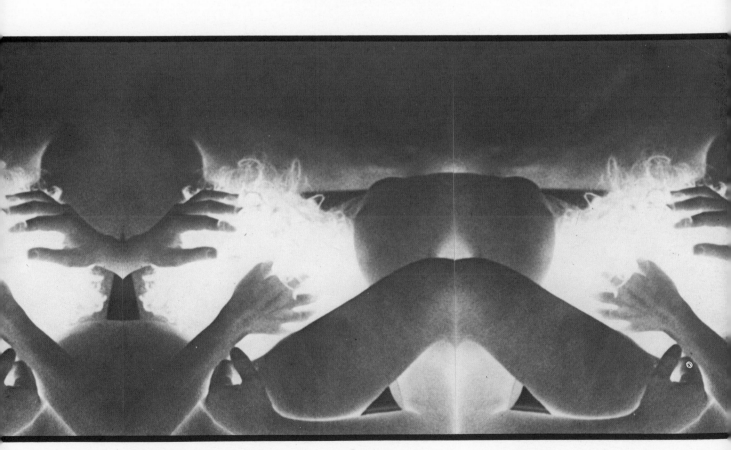

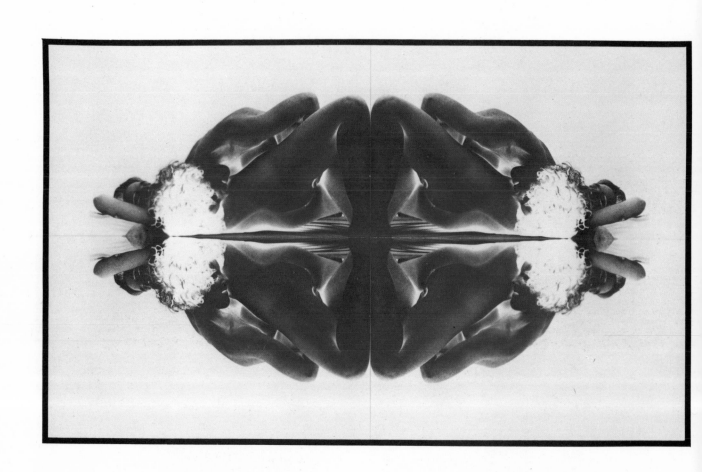

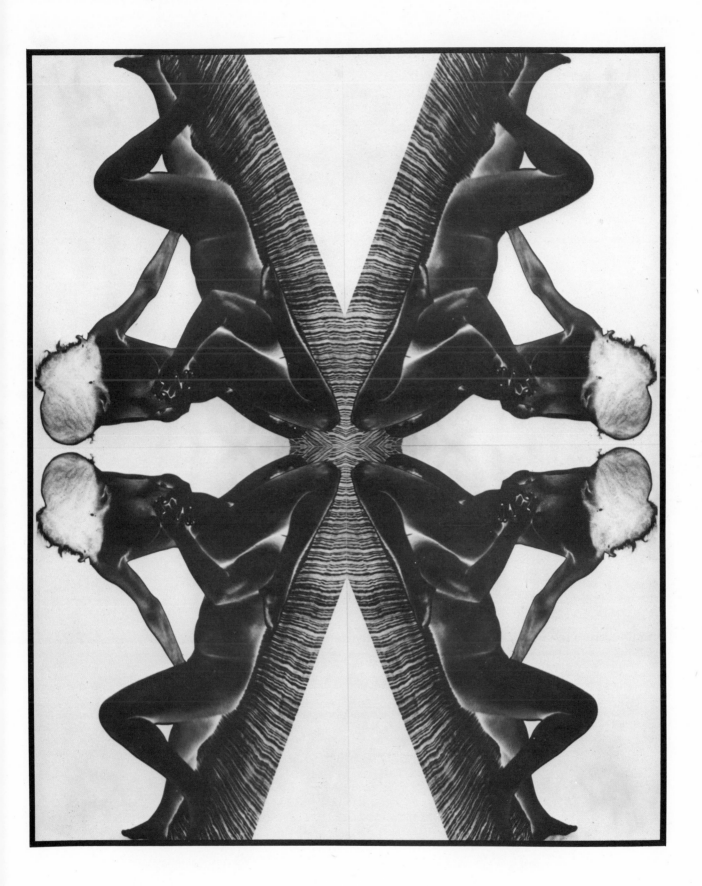

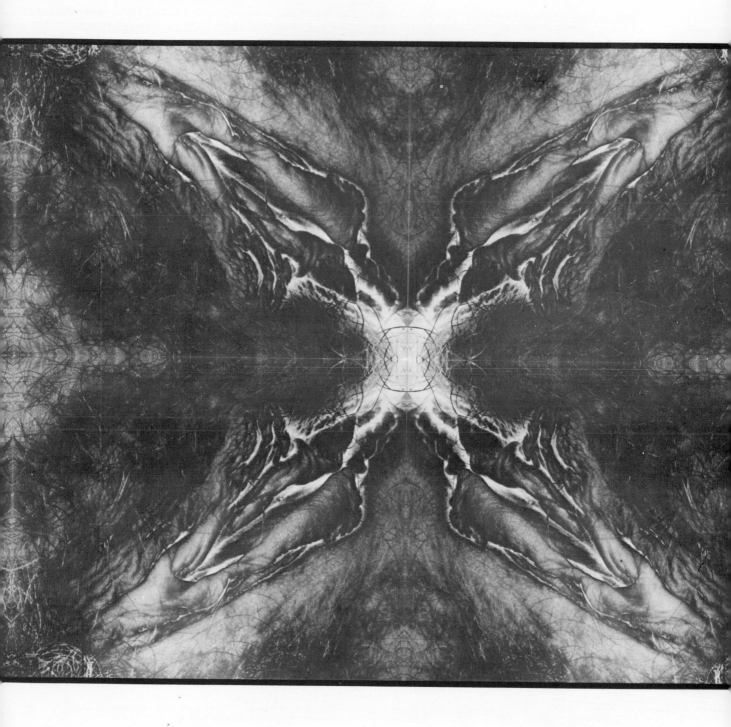

54

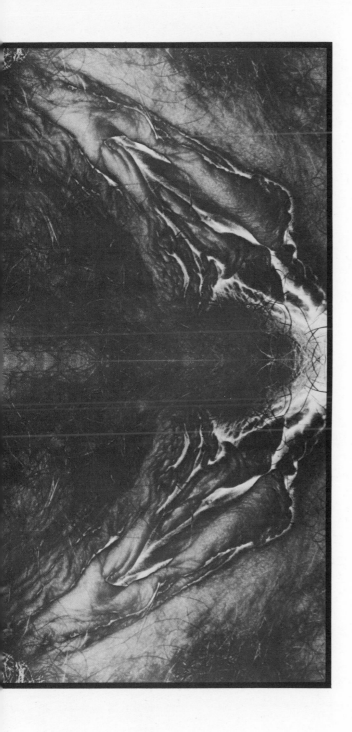

VII

Clitoris
Navel
Plexus
Psyche

**Each dwelling shall begin with the self
firmly planted on her own spot
concentrating energy**

Point
Spiral
Helix

**Stretching, unfolding, expanding
turning, whirling
outward upon her axis**

56

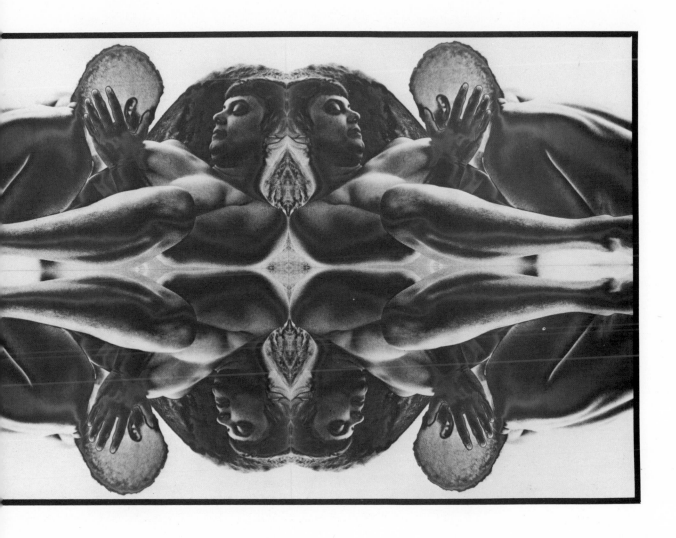

Ears
Nostrils
Mouth
Vagina
Anus

Each orifice dilates, opening
like windows, the air
dances through the body

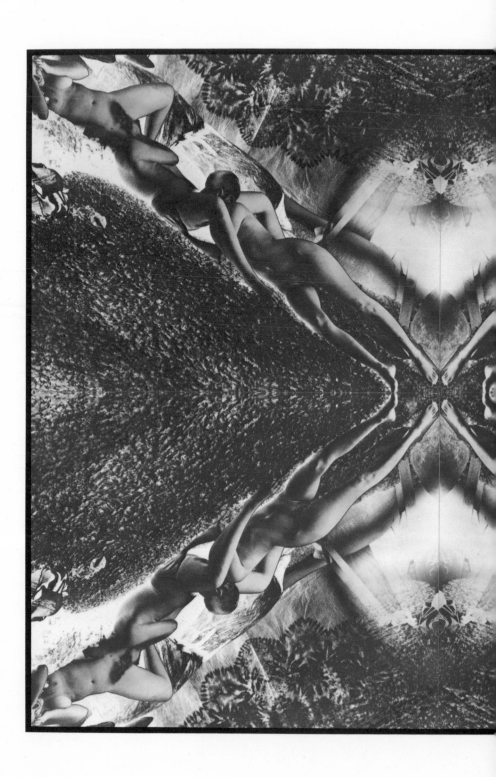

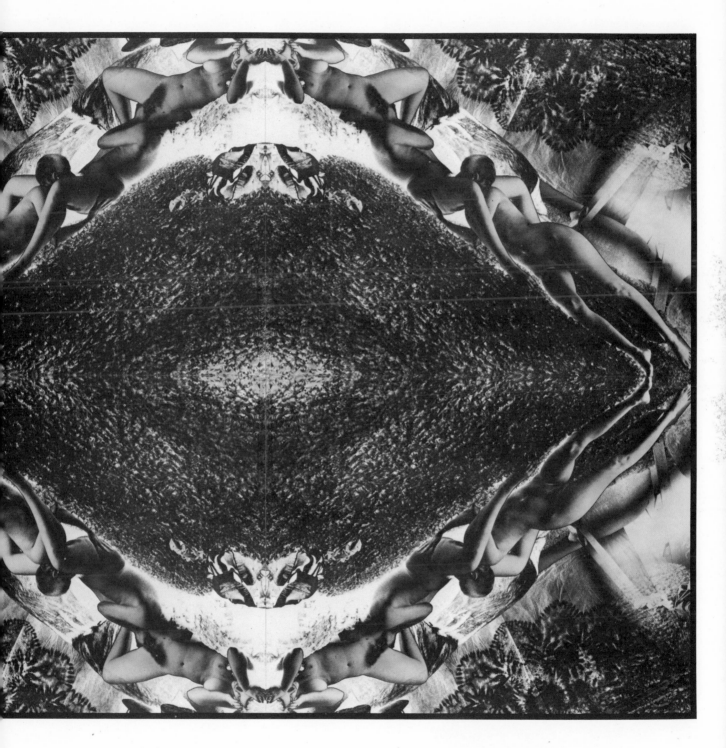

We revolve round one another
like stars   sharing
electrons   women
becoming
matter

and we shall build the city
without walls

Publications of
THE NAIAD PRESS, INC.
P.O. Box 10543 ● Tallahassee, FL 32302

Mail orders welcome. Please include 15% postage.

Contract with the World by Jane Rule. A novel. 340 pp.
ISBN 0-930044-28-2 $7.95

Yantras of Womanlove by Tee A. Corinne.
64 pp. ISBN 0-930044-304 $6.95

Mrs. Porter's Letter by Vicki P. McConnell. A novel.
220 pp. ISBN 0-930044-29-0 $6.95

To the Cleveland Station by Carol Anne Douglas. A novel.
192 pp. ISBN 0-930044-27-4 $6.95

The Nesting Place by Sarah Aldridge. A novel. 224 pp.
ISBN 0-930044-26-6 $6.95

This Is Not for You by Jane Rule. A novel. 284 pp.
ISBN 0-930044-25-8 $7.95

Faultline by Sheila Ortiz Taylor. A novel. 140 pp.
ISBN 0-930044-24-X $6.95

The Lesbian in Literature by Barbara Grier. 3rd ed.
Foreword by Maida Tilchen. A comprehensive bibliog.
240 pp. ISBN 0-930044-23-1   ind. $7.95
inst. $10.00

Anna's Country by Elizabeth Lang. A novel. 208 pp.
ISBN 0-930044-19-3 $6.95

Lesbian Writer: Collected Work of Claudia Scott
edited by Frances Hanckel and Susan Windle. Poetry. 128 pp.
ISBN 0-930044-22-3 $4.50

Prism by Valerie Taylor. A novel. 158 pp.
ISBN 0-930044-18-5 $6.95

Black Lesbians: An Annotated Bibliography compiled by
JR Roberts. Foreword by Barbara Smith. 112 pp.
ISBN 0-930044-21-5   ind. $5.95
inst. $8.00

The Marquise and the Novice by Victoria Ramstetter.
A novel. 108 pp. ISBN 0-930044-16-9 $4.95

Labiaflowers by Tee A. Corinne. 40 pp. $3.95

Outlander by Jane Rule. Short stories, essays.
207 pp. ISBN 0-930044-17-7 $6.95

Sapphistry: The Book of Lesbian Sexuality by
Pat Califia. 195 pp. ISBN 0-930044-14-2 $6.95

Lesbian-Feminism in Turn-of-the-Century Germany.
An anthology. Translated and edited by Lillian Faderman
and Brigitte Eriksson. 120 pp. ISBN 0-930044-13-4 $5.95

(continued on next page)

The Black and White of It by Ann Allen Shockley.
Short stories. 112 pp. ISBN 0-930044-15-0 $5.95

At the Sweet Hour of Hand-in-Hand by Renée Vivien.
Translated by Sandia Belgrade. Poetry. xix, 81 pp.
ISBN 0-930044-11-8 $5.50

All True Lovers by Sarah Aldridge. A novel. 292 pp.
ISBN 0-930044-10-X $6.95

A Woman Appeared to Me by Renée Vivien. Translated
by Jeannette H. Foster. A novel. xxxi, 65 pp.
ISBN 0-930044-06-1 $5.00

Lesbiana by Barbara Grier. Book reviews from
The Ladder. iv, 309 pp. ISBN 0-930044-05-3 $5.00

The Muse of the Violets by Renée Vivien. Translated
byMargaret Porter and Catharine Kroger. Poetry.
xiv, 70 pp. ISBN 0-930044-07-X $4.00

Cytherea's Breath by Sarah Aldridge. A novel. 240 pp.
ISBN 0-930044-02-9 $6.95

Tottie by Sarah Aldridge. A novel. 181 pp.
ISBN 0-930044-01-0 $5.95

The Latecomer by Sarah Aldridge. A novel. 107 pp.
ISBN 0-930044-00-2 $5.00